© 1997 Published by: The Bluecoat Press,
Bluecoat Chambers, School Lane, Liverpool, L1 3BX

Photographs appear courtesy of the Board of
Trustees of the National Museums and Galleries
on Merseyside

Front cover: *Saxonia* and *Reina Del Pacifico*, Liverpool
Back cover: *Caronia* in Gladstone Graving Dock, 1951
(Cover photographs from the University of
Liverpool Special Collections)

Designed by: Graham Nuttall
Origination by: Primary Four
Printed by: GZ Printek

Acknowledgments

Unless otherwise stated all photographs are from the Stewart Bale Archive at the Merseyside Maritime Museum. Ephemera is from the Maritime Archives collections.

All material reproduced from Merseyside Maritime Museum collections remains the copyright of the Board of Trustees of the National Museums & Galleries on Merseyside.

Many ships were refitted. The passenger accommodation was altered throughout their service; however all data, unless otherwise stated, is correct for the vessel at the date of build.

Special thanks should go to Peter Kenyon, David Eccles and Norman West, members of the Liverpool Nautical Research Society whose assistance in the compilation of this anthology is warmly appreciated.

Karen Howard
Curator of Photographic Archives Project, Merseyside Maritime Museum.

LIVERPOOL LINERS

KAREN HOWARD

The Bluecoat Press

Foreword

It was as the premier port for Europe to USA and Canada that Liverpool held the world's headlines for nearly a century.

In mid-Atlantic, the royalty and nobility of the Old World met the film stars and nouveau riche of the New. Financial grandees like the Morgans and go-getters like the Vanderbilts searching for ducal spouses for their daughters, lounged or revelled the nights away in floating palaces whose very names sounded more like a romantic fantasy land than motorised steel boxes tossed on the grey ocean.

While on board, these saloon passengers inhabited their own elite world of grandeur and luxury, in surroundings imitating the opulence they knew or aspired to, modelled on the splendours of Versailles or even Ancient Rome. These tycoons relaxed from the pace of business and enjoyed without let or hindrance, the good things of life!

On the underside of this super structure of grandeur were the swarms of emigrants, filling the third class, with its sparsely furnished cabins and communal rooms, (though compared with the days of sail, it was truly palatial) the sweating 'black gang' feeding the boilers, the deckhands, stewards and other minions keeping the wheels turning.

'One picture is worth a thousand words'. For an increasing number of us now, these days are not even a memory. They are a world almost beyond our ability to imagine, so much has the pattern of life changed.

These photographs, mostly taken by Stewart Bale, the acknowledged doyen of industrial photographers of Merseyside, along with some by other photographers, give us an unequalled glimpse of these 'floating palaces'.

Gordon Read
Curator of Archives, Merseyside Maritime Museum.

Cunard S.S. Co Ltd. • 31,550t • Built 1906 John Brown & Co. Ltd, Glasgow • Passenger Accommodation: 563 1st class; 464 2nd class; 1,138 3rd class.

Lusitania, Sandon Dock, Liverpool 1907
(MDHB Archive, Merseyside Maritime Museum)

Until the turn of the 20th century, the Cunard Line had been a major force in transatlantic passenger travel. By the end of the 1900s though, Cunard's ships were looking decidedly dated, particularly in the light of burgeoning German competition.

The British Government became persuaded that in time of war, very few, if any, merchant vessels would be suitable for requisition, particularly since the White Star fleet had been acquired by the American railroad magnate J.P. Morgan. After several years of discussions, Cunard managed to negotiate an Admiralty subsidy for the building of the *Mauretania*, *Lusitania* and *Aquitania*.

The *Lusitania* was the largest ship in the world. Sadly her outstanding service record, during which in 1909 she made a westward North Atlantic crossing in 4 days, 11 hours, 42 minutes, is often overshadowed by her dramatic loss in 1915.

A condition of the Admiralty loan had been that all three new liners were fitted with decks that could hold gun mountings. During wartime they would serve as auxiliary cruisers. However, early into the 1914-1918 War, the *Lusitania* ran the West Atlantic mail route and continued to sail her usual service once a month. That is, until her interception by a U-Boat off the southern coast of Ireland. The facts surrounding the incident remain contentious to this day.

Aquitania, Landing Stage, Liverpool 1919
(MDHB Archive, Merseyside Maritime Museum)

Cunard S.S. Co Ltd. • 31,550t • Built 1914 John Brown & Co. Ltd, Glasgow • Passenger Accommodation: 618 1st class; 614 2nd class; 1,998 3rd class • 972 crew

Along with the earlier _Lusitania_, the _Aquitania_ was the floating embodiment of luxurious opulence. The decorative assortment of public rooms mirrored the interior decor of stately homes and smart apartments on either side of the Atlantic.

The _Aquitania_ enjoyed 40 years of transatlantic passenger trade as well as active war service. Pictured here, she dwarfs the Wallasey 'Luggage Boat' alongside the Stage.

Ocean S.S. Co. Ltd. • 11,321t • Built 1923 Cammell Laird & Co. Ltd., Birkenhead • Passenger accommodation: 155 1st class • 80 crew

Designed for the Far Eastern passenger trade, the *Sarpedon* had 1st class accommodation throughout. Never a commercial success, she was moved to the Australian service in 1946 and eventually broken up in 1953. She is seen here on sailing day, flying both the Blue Peter and the Pilot's Flag, with the Cunarder *Scythia* in the background.

Sarpedon, Landing Stage, Liverpool 1923
(MDHB Archive, Merseyside Maritime Museum)

White Star Liner, Landing Stage, Liverpool 1923 (MDHB Archive, Merseyside Maritime Museum)
This could be the *Celtic*, built in 1901. She is dressed overall though the reason for this is not immediately apparent.

Ocean Steam Navigation Co. Ltd. (White Star Line) • 26,943t • Built 1930 Harland & Wolff Ltd., Belfast • Passenger accommodation: 498 3rd class; 504 cabin class; 551 tourist class • 500 crew

M.V. Britannic set a trend as a diesel-propelled liner, followed two years later by the *Georgic*. Her low superstructure and flat funnels (the forward funnel was in fact a dummy used to house radio equipment) were quite distinctive. *Britannic* arrived in Liverpool in June 1930 to set sail for her maiden voyage to New York.

Britannic, Liverpool 1930

(MDHB Archive, Merseyside Maritime Museum)

9

Duchess of Bedford, Liverpool 1928 — Canadian Pacific Railway Co. • 20,123t • Built 1928 John Brown & Co. Ltd., Glasgow • Passenger accommodation: 510 3rd class; 580 cabin class; 480 tourist class • 510 crew
At the Landing Stage.

DUCHESS OF BEDFORD. — Entrance Hall. "A" Deck.

Public rooms such as this would have been common shipboard meeting places. The revolving doors, actually quite an unusual feature, probably helped to protect passengers against the North Atlantic weather.

Duchess of Bedford,
'A' Deck Entrance Hall 1928

Duchess of Bedford, Liverpool 1928
A view from the bridge, looking towards the stern along the starboard side. Notice the triple chime whistles on both the funnels.

Scythia, Deck Scene c.1934

Reina del Pacifico, Lounge 1931

Pacific Steam Navigation Co. • 17,705t • Built 1931 Harland & Wolff Ltd., Belfast • Passenger accommodation: 280 1st class; 162 2nd class; 446 3rd class

The place allocations visible on each chair back would have been given to passengers at the outset of each voyage. This would have assisted the stewards, particularly in noticing who bestowed generous tips.

Reina del Pacifico,
Dining Room 1931

Ulster Monarch 1929   Belfast S.S. Co. Ltd. (Coast Lines) • 3,735t • Built 1929 Harland & Wolff Ltd., Belfast
Starboard bow view at anchor.
Ulster Monarch served as an Irish Sea ferry sailing from Princes Dock, Liverpool, to Belfast.

Ulster Monarch, Bar 1929

Ivernia   Cunard White Star • 21,717t • Built 1955 John Brown & Co. Ltd., Glasgow • Passenger accommodation: 110 1st class; 833 tourist class • 461 crew

(University of Liverpool Special Collections)   A regular on the Liverpool to Montreal service, in 1963 the *Ivernia* was painted green and renamed the *Franconia*.

Franconia
(University of Liverpool Special Collections)

Caronia   Cunard White Star • 34 183t • Built 1948 John Brown & Co. Ltd., Glasgow • Passenger accommodation: 581 1st class; 351 cabin class • 600 crew

   (University of Liverpool Special Collections)   A cruise service supplemented *Caronia's* Southampton to New York run. She was modernised in 1965.

Caronia
(University of Liverpool Special Collections)

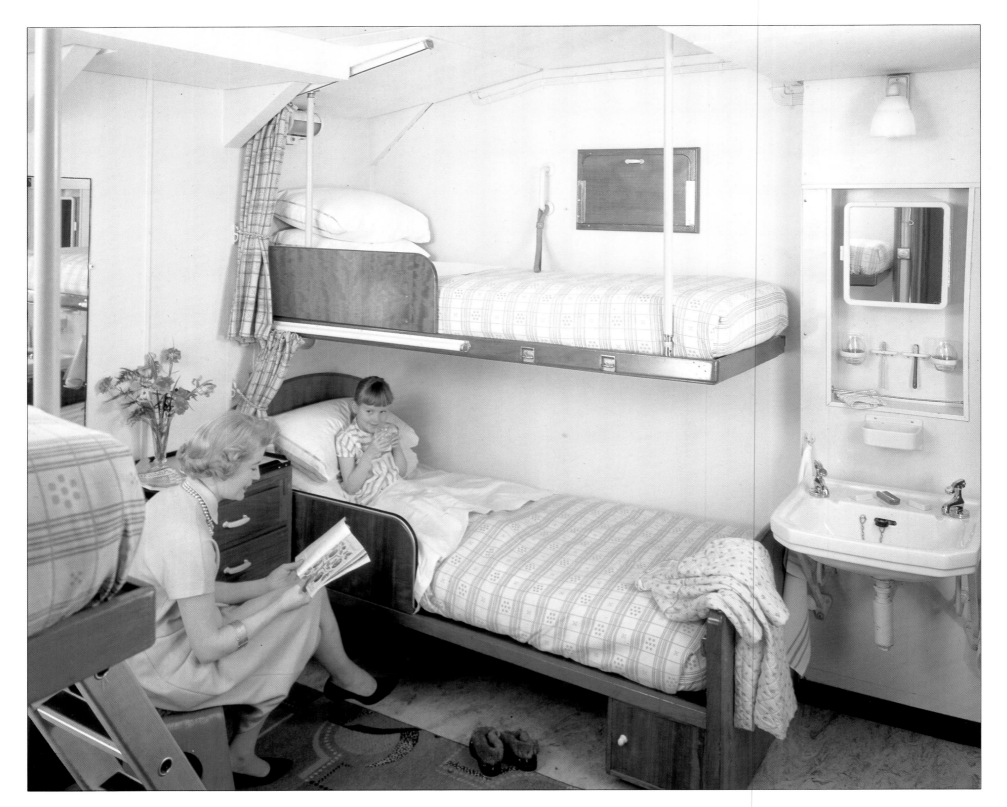

Ivernia

(University of Liverpool Special Collections)

Caronia

Caronia

(University of Liverpool Special Collections)

Caronia

Ivernia

(University of Liverpool Special Collections)

Ivernia

Left: White Star poster advertising the *Titanic*, design by Montague Black about 1912
Centre: White Star Line poster
Right: Cunard Line poster

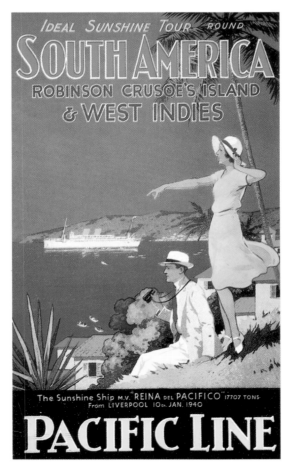

Left: Lamport Holt Line poster
Centre: Pacific Line poster
Right: Blue Funnel Line poster

CANADIAN PACIFIC IN THE ROCKIES

Top: Canadian Pacific voyage memorabilia
Bottom: Cunard White Star luggage labels

Ivernia

(University of Liverpool Special Collections)

Saxonia
(University of Liverpool Special Collections)

Cunard White Star • 21 637t • Built 1954 John Brown & Co. Ltd., Glasgow • Passenger accommodation: 110 1st class; 819 tourist class • 461 crew.
Saxonia ran Cunard's transatlantic service between Liverpool and New York until the early sixties when she, too, was refitted and painted green. The new cruiser was named *Carmania*.

Reina del Pacifico, Lounge 1931
The *Reina del Pacifico* sailed between
Liverpool and the west coast of South
America, reflected in the Spanish Colonial
atmosphere of the public rooms. The lounge
with its minstrels' gallery boasts a particularly
high deckhead which probably extended
through two levels.

Britannic

(University of Liverpool Special Collections)

Empress of Britain,
Midships Funnel by night 1931

Mauretania,
Gladstone Dock, Liverpool 1939

Cunard White Star • 35,738t • Built 1939 Cammell Laird & Co. Ltd., Birkenhead • Passenger accommodation: 470 3rd class; 440 cabin class; 450 tourist class • 780 crew

The North Atlantic passenger trade was badly affected by the Depression of the 1930s. Both Cunard and White Star suffered; so much so that, in the early thirties, the hull of Cunarder S.S. 534 (later to be named _Queen Mary_) lay rusting in John Brown's Glasgow shipyard. On the strong advice of the British Government, Cunard and White Star merged in 1934. A substantial Admiralty loan funded the completion of the _Queen Mary_ and the building of _Mauretania_ and the later _Queen Elizabeth_.

As with earlier ships built with public money, _Mauretania_ was expected to take part in war service if necessary. Indeed, after very few North Atlantic voyages, she was painted grey and given gun mountings. _Mauretania_ could accommodate 7,124 troops; rather less comfortably, it must be assumed, than her usual 1,360 passengers.

After 1945 she mainly sailed from Southampton, but continued to visit Liverpool annually for repairs and a general overhaul.

Horses continued to be used for haulage purposes until well after the 1939-1945 War. The lifeboats were built by Hugh McClean & Sons Ltd. at Shieldhall Dock, Glasgow and could have been transported to Birkenhead by a coaster vessel before being transferred to horse and cart.

Lifeboats for **Mauretania**, Birkenhead 1937

Stepping the Foremast of **Mauretania**,
Cammell Laird Shipbuilding Yard,
Birkenhead 1937
The mast is swung around by one of the
Mersey Docks & Harbour Board's floating
cranes. In the background is a United Molasses
tanker; this company was later to be renamed
the Athel Line.

Stepping the Foremast of **Mauretania**,
Cammell Laird Shipbuilding Yard,
Birkenhead 1937
Also pictured here is the Ellerman ship *City of Pittsburg* which was torpedoed during the 1939-1945 War.

Mauretania, 1st Class Dining Room 1939
Decorative panelling, tapestries, paintings
and glasswork were distinctive features of
1930s liner interiors.

Cunard S.S. Co. Ltd. • 19,680t • Built 1922 Swan Hunter & Wigham Richardson Ltd., Newcastle • Passenger accommodation: 340 1st class; 340 2nd class; 1,500 3rd class • 410 crew

Laconia 1938

Alteration and reduction of the passenger accommodation in 1924 prepared the *Laconia* for the cruise service she operated throughout most of the thirties.

Her wartime sinking in 1942, with 800 Italian prisoners of war amongst those on board, and the subsequent rescue operation, led to what became known as the 'Laconia Order'. This forbade the rescue of survivors of sunken ships. Later British prosecutors at the Nüremberg Trials sited the 'Laconia Order' as a virtual act of murder.

Adriatic 1929

Ocean Steam Navigation Co. Ltd. (White Star Line) • 24,541t
• Built 1906 Harland & Wolff Ltd., Belfast • Passenger
accommodation: 425 1st class; 500 2nd class; 1,900 steerage
• 557 crew

Although *Adriatic's* first commercial voyage
was from Southampton to New York, she
then returned to Liverpool, the departure
port of her maiden voyage, for regular
sailings across the North Atlantic.

It is debatable what level of protection this elegant frame alongside the bed could have afforded against a rough Atlantic crossing.

Adriatic, 1st Class Cabin 1929

Georgic, Lounge 1932

Oceanic Steam Navigation Co. Ltd. (White Star Line) • 27,759t • Built 1932 Harland & Wolff Ltd., Belfast • Passenger accommodation: 506 3rd class; 479 cabin class; 557 tourist class

Georgic 1932

Possibly a Cocktail Lounge. The *Georgic*, along with her sister ship Britannic, was the largest motorship of her time. She generally sailed between Liverpool and New York, however, in 1939, under the gathering clouds of war, she ran a four day '4th of July Cruise' from New York to Halifax, Nova Scotia.

Ausonia, Cabin 1938

Cunard S.S. Co. Ltd. • 13,912t Built 1921 Armstrong
Whitworth Co. Ltd., Newcastle • Passenger accommodation:
1,178 3rd class; 510 cabin class • 270 crew
Notice the single tap at the basin. Only cold
running water was available in the cabins;
this couple would have hot water brought to
them by a steward.

Ausonia, Dining Room 1938
The bare steel deckhead suggests that this may have been tourist class accommodation, which was added to the *Ausonia* during the 1930s. Indeed the re-fit could have been the occasion of this series of photographs.
In 1942 the *Ausonia* was converted into a Royal Navy repair ship.

Ausonia, Gymnasium 1938
This is undoubtedly a publicity shot; the men dressed in white being Physical Training Instructors. Shipboard gym equipment would have included bars, exercise bicycles, medicine balls and 'automatic camels'.

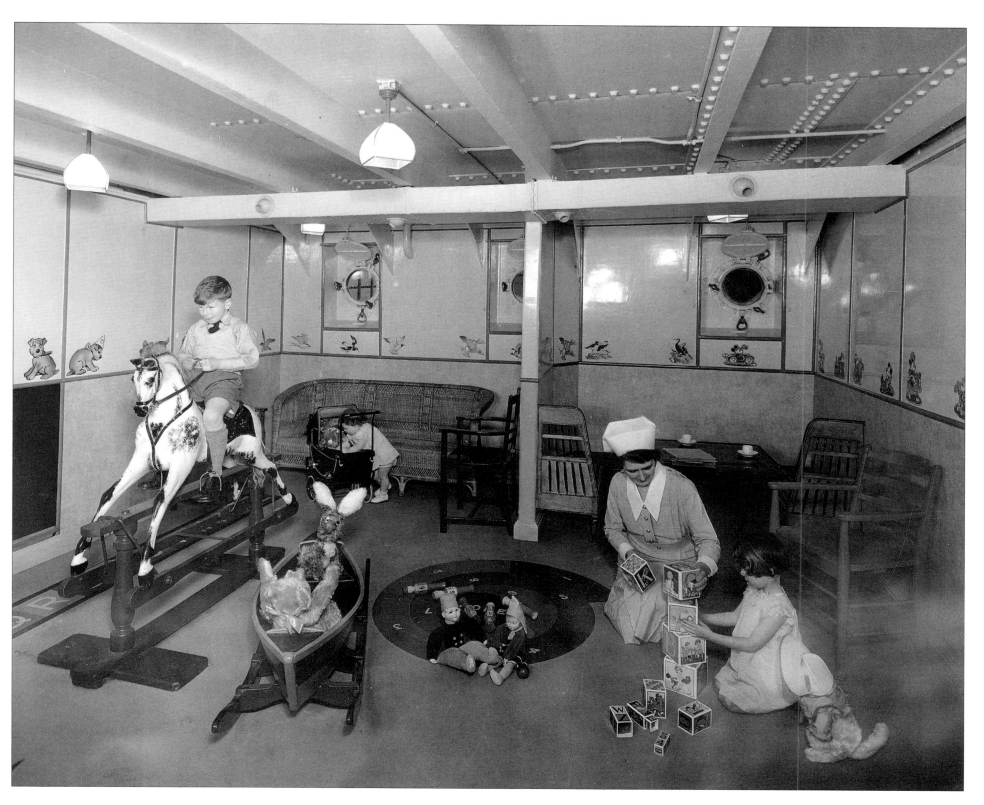

A nurse would always be in attendance in the playroom. Decor was highly durable with rubber flooring and rather basic furnishing, ensuring minimum wear and tear.

Ausonia,
Children's Playroom 1938

***Accra II*,**
1st Class Lounge 1939

Elder Dempster Lines Ltd. (British & African Steam Navigation Co. Ltd.) • 9,337t • Built 1926 Harland & Wolff Ltd., Belfast • Passenger accommodation: 243 1st class; 76 2nd class
The Colonial decor is well suited to the West African service that the *Accra II* sailed until she sank in 1940, a casualty of the War.

By the 1930s, interior decor of transatlantic liners had moved away from traditional styles and tended towards a contemporary, sleek Art Deco influence.
An exception, however, could often be found in the Smoke Room. Styled in a heavier, more traditional manner, such rooms exuded a staid atmosphere reminiscent of a 'Gentlemen's Club'.

Accra II,
1st Class Smoke Room 1939

Accra II, 1st Class Cabin 1939
The exquisite bed linen contrasts rather sharply with the racking on the deck and over the steel bulkhead. Perhaps this was recently converted or even temporary accommodation. This series of photographs was taken whilst the *Accra* was berthed in South West Brunswick Dock, Liverpool.

Cunard S.S.Co.Ltd. • 14,013t • Built 1925 Armstrong Whitworth Co. Ltd., Newcastle • Passenger accommodation: 1,200 3rd class; 500 cabin class • 270 crew

This type of accommodation was undoubtedly occupied by emigrant passengers, the 'bread and butter' of the transatlantic passenger trade. The travellers whose money, in effect, kept the great passenger liners afloat, unfortunately did not experience many of their comforts. Often four fifths of the passengers would be squeezed into one third of the ship.

Emigrants on board the *Ascania* would have been bound for Canada as she sailed from Liverpool to the St. Lawrence River, reaching Montreal during the summer but turning around at St. John's, New Brunswick, in winter.

Ascania,
Dormitory Accommodation 1947

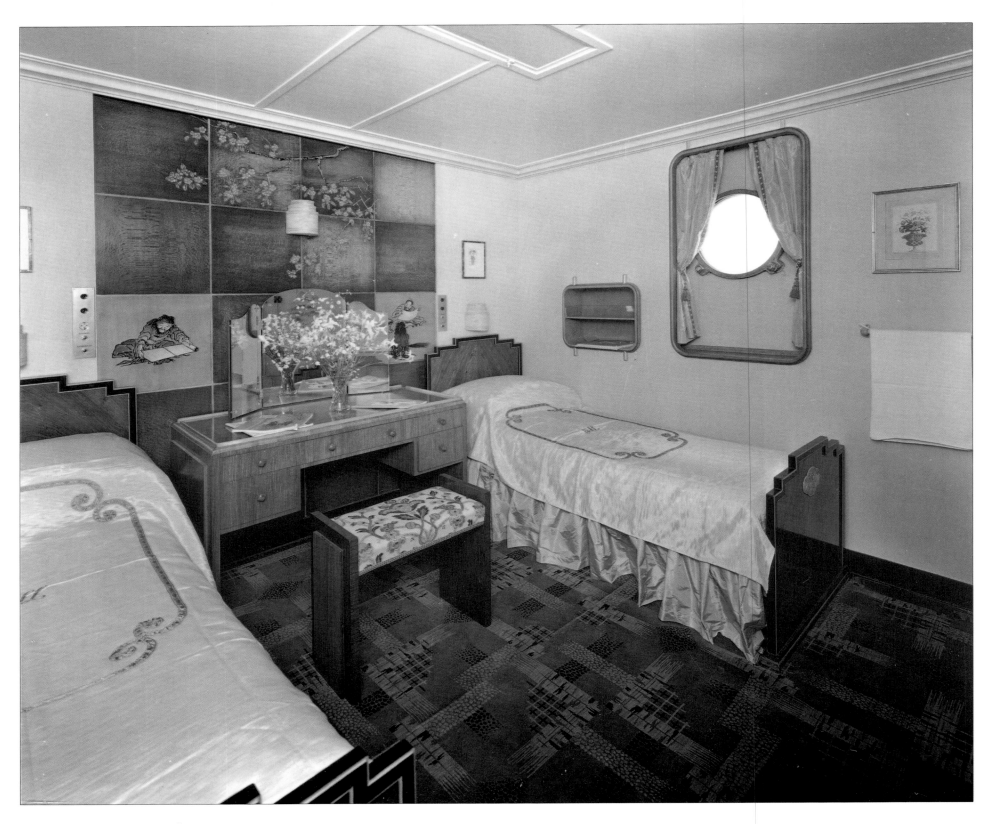

Georgic, Cabin 1932

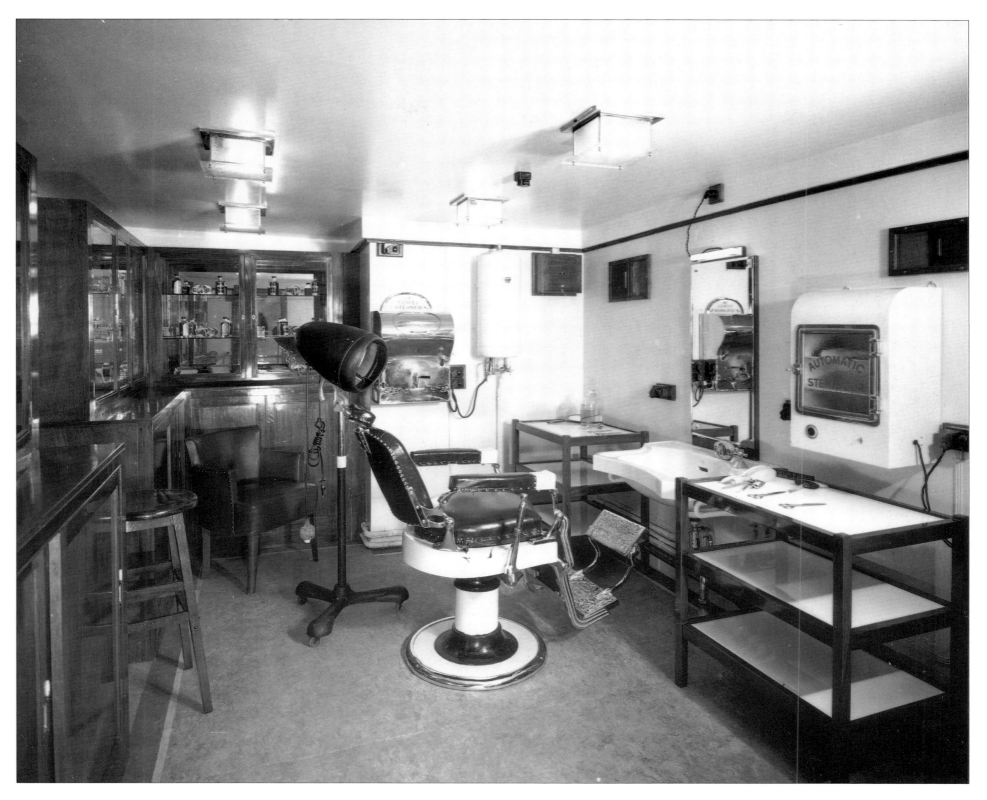

Ellerman Hall Line Ltd. • 10,902t • Built 1922 Swan Hunter & Wigham Richardson Ltd., Newcastle • Passenger accommodation: 230 1st class; 100 2nd class • 190 crew
City of Paris ran the Liverpool to Bombay service.

City of Paris,
Barber Shop 1948

Aurania 1938
Cunard S.S. Co. Ltd. • 13,984t • Built 1924 Swan Hunter &
Wigham Richardson Ltd., Newcastle • Passenger
accommodation: 500 cabin class; 1,200 3rd class • 270 crew
**Built for the Liverpool to Montreal service,
the _Aurania_ was converted to a repair ship
in 1942 and renamed _HMS Artifex_.**

Ocean Steam Navigation Co. Ltd. (White Star Line) • 23,884t • Built 1904 Harland & Wolff Ltd., Belfast • Passenger accommodation: 425 1st class; 450 2nd class; 2,000 steerage

Baltic 1929

At the time of her Maiden Voyage from Liverpool to New York, the *Baltic* was the largest ship in the world.

Franconia,
1st Class Dining Room 1936

Cunard S.S. Co. Ltd. • 20,155t • Built 1923 John Brown & Co. Ltd., Glasgow • Passenger accommodation: 221 1st class; 356 2nd class; 1,266 3rd class • 414 crew

The _Franconia_ sailed between Liverpool and New York from 1923- 1933, supplementing this service with winter cruises.
In 1930 cabin and tourist classes of accommodation were added. During 1934 she sailed briefly from Southampton but resumed Liverpool departures in 1935, and was broken up at Inverkeithing in 1957.

Staffordshire 1929

Bibby Line Ltd. • 10,654t • Built 1929 Fairfield Steam Boat &
Engineering Co. Ltd., Glasgow • Passenger accommodation:
273 1st class • 200 crew

This area would have provided refuge from
the tropical heat encountered on a sailing
from Liverpool to Burma.

All Bibby Line ships were named after
English counties and a fine model of the
Staffordshire is housed at the Merseyside
Maritime Museum.

Stratheden 1937   P&O S.S. Co. • 23,722t • Built 1937 Vickers Armstrongs Ltd., Barrow • Passenger accommodation: 448 1st class; 563 tourist class

Along with *Strathallen*, *Stratheden* was commissioned for the Australian passenger trade in a bid to challenge the *Orion* and *Orcades* of the Orient Lines. In comparison to the imposing interiors of earlier liners, the decor of the *Stratheden* was decidedly restrained.

Stratheden was later bought by Cunard for the Canadian service and was eventually scrapped in Italy during the late 1960s.

Canadian Pacific Railway Co. • 19,379t • Built 1924 Cammell Laird & Co. Ltd., Birkenhead • Passenger accommodation: 220 1st class; 444 tourist class

Empress of Australia 1953

The second *Empress of Australia* was initially built for French owners De Grasse. However, in 1953, she was bought by Canadian Pacific for the North Atlantic service. She is seen here on sailing day, with an Alexandra Towing Company tender, possibly the *Egerton*. The Royal Mail flag denotes that she is carrying mail.

In the background, an Isle of Man passenger ferry can just be seen.

Aquitania, River Mersey, Liverpool

Cunard S.S. Co Ltd. • 45,647t • Built 1914 John Brown & Co. Ltd, Glasgow • Passenger Accommodation: 618 1st class; 614 2nd class; 1,998 3rd class • 972 crew

Cunard White Star • 21,637t • Built 1954 John Brown & Co. Ltd., Glasgow • Passenger accommodation: 110 1st class; 189 tourist class • 461 crew

Saxonia ran Cunard's transatlantic service between Liverpool and New York until the early sixties when she, too, was refitted and painted green. The new cruiser was named *Carmania*.

Saxonia, Liverpool

(University of Liverpool Special Collections)

Empress of Britain, 1st Class suite 1931

Canadian Pacific Railway Co. • 42,348t • Built 1931 John Brown & Co. Ltd., Glasgow • Passenger accommodation: 465 1st class; 470 3rd class; 260 tourist class • 740 crew

The second *Empress of Britain* (an earlier ship was built in 1906) was ordered by Canadian Pacific in 1928 in a bid to lure passenger trade away from New York. She was the largest vessel on the Canadian service, sailing to Chicago via Montreal. At an average speed of 24 knots, this was actually quicker than the Liverpool to New York run. Unfortunately, the service did not prove popular and the *Empress of Britain* become probably the least profitable liner of her time.

During the winter, she ran 1st class world cruises on which passenger numbers were reduced to a mere seven hundred. This meant that travellers enjoyed almost unrivalled comfort and service.